The Twilight Realm

Aliens

Please visit our website, **www.garethstevens.com**. For a free color catalog of all our high-quality books, call toll free 1-800-542-2595 or fax 1-877-542-2596.

Publisher Cataloging Data

Pipe, Jim, 1966–
    Aliens / Jim Pipe.
    p.   cm. – (The twilight realm)
Includes bibliographical references and index.
Summary: This book examines reported encounters with alien beings including
UFOs, alien abductions, government cover-ups, and more.
Contents: We are not alone-- – UFO alert! – Close encounters – Alien
abduction – UFO down! – Men in black – War of the worlds – Riddles and mysteries – Ancient astronauts –
Alien science – Watching the skies – Twilight quiz.
        ISBN 978-1-4339-8747-2 (hard bound) – ISBN 978-1-4339-8748-9 (pbk.)
ISBN 978-1-4339-8749-6 (6-pack)
        1. Unidentified flying objects—Juvenile literature   2. Human-alien encounters—Juvenile
literature   3. Extraterrestrial beings—Juvenile literature
[1. Unidentified flying objects   2. Human-alien encounters   3. Extraterrestrial beings]
I. Title
            2013
    001.942—dc23   2012038517

Published in 2013 by
Gareth Stevens Publishing
111 East 14th Street, Suite 349
New York, NY 10003

Produced for Gareth Stevens by Wayland a division of Hachette Children's Books
a Hachette UK company
www.hachette.co.uk

Editor: Paul Manning
Designer: Paul Manning

Picture Credits
t=top **b**=bottom
13t, 15b,16b, 18t, 19 (H.G. Wells and Orson Welles), 21: Wikimedia Commons. All other images ©
Shutterstock and Dreamstime.

Printed in the United States of America

CPSIA compliance information: Batch CW13GS: For further information contact Gareth Stevens, New York, New York at 1-800-542-2595.

The Twilight Realm

Aliens

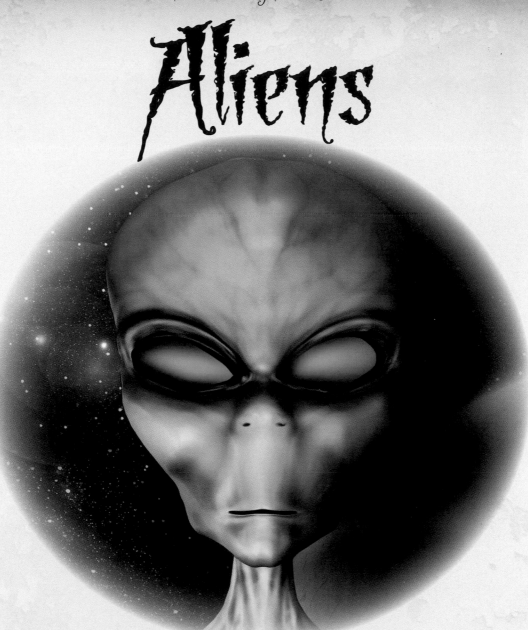

Jim Pipe

Gareth Stevens
Publishing

Contents

We Are Not Alone...

Scientists have long believed that there may be alien life out there somewhere. But have aliens from outer space ever visited Earth? Where do they come from and what do they look like?

Over the past 60 years, there have been thousands of reports of mysterious flying saucers hovering overhead, or bright lights shooting across the night sky. Dozens of people also claim to have met aliens. Some stories are clearly hoaxes, like the "Venusians" met by George Adamski in the California desert in 1953 (we now know that conditions on Venus make it impossible for intelligent life to exist there). But other reports are harder to explain away – like the puzzling nests of flattened reeds that Australian farmer George Pedley said were made by an alien spacecraft in 1966. Unidentified Flying Objects, or UFOs, *do* exist. But are they alien craft, top-secret test planes, or bizarre tricks of the light caused by freak weather conditions?

▼ *In many sightings, aliens are described as small, grey creatures with black, glassy eyes.*

The Quest for ET

Ever since human beings first gazed into the night sky, people have dreamed of discovering life on other planets. But it was not until 1971 that scientists were able to begin listening for radio signals from deep space.

Somewhere out in the vastness of the cosmos, there is every chance that extraterrestrials (ETs) do exist. But it's unlikely we'll get to meet them. The nearest star to our sun, Proxima Centauri, would take our fastest spacecraft about 70,000 years to reach!

But do we really *want* to meet ETs? Suppose that aliens came to wipe us out and take over our planet? Even if they were friendly, they might bring with them diseases that would be deadly for human beings.

▼ *A great place to start looking for intelligent life is on planets outside our solar system. So far, some 540 such planets have been found, many by instruments like this roaming coronograph used in NASA's Kepler mission.*

"I imagine they might exist in massive ships, having used up all the resources from their home planet. Such advanced aliens would perhaps become nomads, looking to conquer and colonize whatever planets they can reach."

Scientist Stephen Hawking on aliens

UFO Alert!

▲ *UFOs are typically described as flat, saucer-like objects swooping through the air. Scientists believe most are really misidentified aircraft or tricks of the light, but a few UFO cases are genuinely baffling.*

UFOs have been seen by pilots, astronauts, sailors – and even two former US presidents, Jimmy Carter and Ronald Reagan (see page 27). Don't take their word for it. Most UFOs are seen by ordinary people taking their dog for a walk or driving along a road. You could be next!

UFOs first hit the headlines in the 1940s. During World War II, many British and US pilots saw glowing balls of light following their planes, which shifted in color from red to orange and white and then back again.

Called "Foo Fighters" by the pilots, these balls of light were speedier than any aircraft. The terrified pilots thought they might be a German secret weapon. Later, people wondered if they were really alien spaceships.

By the 1950s, flying saucers were a major news story. Many were seen with the naked eye, but in 1956, a radar station in Bentwaters, Norfolk, UK, tracked a UFO moving at over 15,000 km/h! In 1976, a jet fighter spotted a UFO over the city of Tehran, Iran, and was about to open fire when its weapons suddenly refused to function. Reports still come in every year of spooky lights in the sky performing aerobatic feats that would be impossible for normal planes.

Yes, most UFOs can be explained away as passing aircraft, satellites, balloons, or strangely-shaped clouds. But about 5 percent remain a mystery. Many are picked up on radar and spotted by trained observers such as pilots, police, and military personnel. Often the evidence is compelling. Even so, it's hard to prove if these UFOs really are piloted by visiting aliens.

"UFO" is a modern term, but people have been spotting weird objects in the sky for centuries. In 1088, a Chinese scholar wrote about a huge flying object that was able to take off at tremendous speed and cast a blinding light for ten miles around!

The First "Flying Saucer"

On June 24, 1947, US pilot Kenneth Arnold was flying a small plane near Mount Rainier, Washington, when he saw a bright flash in the sky. Looking closer, he claims he saw nine V-shaped UFOs traveling at speeds of about 1,000 miles per hour. Arnold later described how the fleet of alien craft flew across a mountain crest like saucers skimming over water.

Arnold's sighting was soon headline news all over the world. Within months, there were hundreds of similar reports of "flying saucers" across America.

▼ Kenneth Arnold holds an artist's impression of the crescent-shaped UFO he saw in 1947. Arnold's description gave rise to the popular term "flying saucer."

Close Encounters

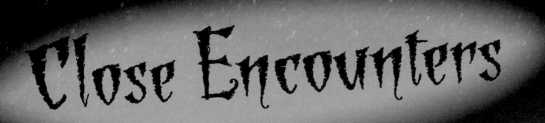

▼ *This giant tower of rock in Wyoming is the scene of an epic meeting between humans and aliens in the 1977 Steven Spielberg film* Close Encounters of the Third Kind.

Imagine driving down a lonely country road at night. Suddenly you're blinded by a dazzling light. The massive bulk of an alien craft blocks the road ahead. Shadowy alien figures emerge and surround you. What do you do? How do you describe your experience to other people?

The term "close encounter" first appeared in the 1970s, when the American UFO expert Dr. Allen J. Hynek came up with a new way of describing alien sightings.

In Hynek's new jargon, the type of sighting that took place in Lubbock, Texas, in 1951, when local people reported mysterious lights whizzing over their town in a V formation, was a "close encounter of the first kind" (CE1). In the second type, a CE2, some physical trace is left behind after the sighting – such as tracks on the ground or flattened crops. When aliens are spotted, it's a CE3 – as in the tale of policeman Lonnie Zamora.

In April 1964, Zamora was driving along a road in New Mexico, when he claims he saw a silvery object on four legs. Spooked by Zamora's car, two small figures nearby hopped into the spacecraft. It immediately took off with a mighty roar, leaving behind patches of scorched earth.

Attack of the Goblins

UFO sightings can be frightening enough, but imagine encountering aliens face to face!

On August 21, 1955, Kentucky farmer Billy Ray Taylor and his wife were visiting their friend Lucky Sutton when Taylor claims he saw a "large shining disc" land nearby. When he ran to tell the Suttons, they laughed at him. But after Sutton's dog began barking, both men went to investigate – and reportedly saw a hideous goblin-like creature heading towards them.

Terrified, the men ran back inside. Soon, other creatures were swarming over the roof and peering in through the windows. Shooting at them had no effect. After several hours under siege, the Sutton and Taylor families fled in two cars to the local police station. Though investigators looked for evidence, no trace of the landing or the aliens was ever found.

▲ The alien "goblins" seen at the Sutton farm were said to have upright pointed ears, flat noses, thin limbs, and clawlike hands.

"It was a serious thing to him. … It was fresh in his mind until the day he died. He never cracked a smile when he told the story…. He got pale and you could see it in his eyes. He was scared to death."

Lucky Sutton's daughter, Geraldine Hawkins

11

Alien Abduction

Tales of people being kidnapped by aliens are not as rare as you might think. Often they are dramatic, detailed – and freaky!

On November 5, 1975, 18-year-old logger Travis Walton was heading home from work in the forests of Arizona when he and his workmates saw what they described as a large, glowing disc hovering above a clearing. When Walton walked closer, he claims that a blue-green ray from the craft blasted him backwards. Thinking he was dead, his friends fled the scene. When they returned later, Walton had vanished.

Five days later, Walton turned up in a nearby town, claiming to have been abducted by aliens. Two doctors examined him, but found nothing unusual. At the spot where Walton had been zapped by the ray, police found no signs of burning. Yet, under hypnosis, Walton gave detailed, vivid descriptions of his alien captors and their spacecraft. He still stands by his story today.

► Dazzling lights, strange sounds, terrifying sensations – but is the nightmare of alien abduction real or imagined?

An Alien Starchart?

In September 1961, US couple Betty and Barney Hill were driving home through New Hampshire when they reported seeing a giant UFO ahead. It loomed closer until it floated right above them. They felt a tingling sensation – then everything went blank.

When they awoke the next morning, they found curious marks on their bodies and a strange pink powder on Betty's dress. They also realized they had lost two hours.

Days later, Betty began to have troubled dreams in which she met aliens on board a spacecraft. The aliens appeared as human-like figures about 5 feet tall, with greyish skin and "wraparound" eyes.

Betty drew a chart, which she claims the aliens had shown her on the spaceship. It showed a star system in another part of the galaxy. Incredibly, this group of stars, Zeta Reticuli, was not discovered by astronomers until eight years later!

▲ After her reported alien encounter, Betty described having nightmares in which aliens carried out medical tests on her. They cut off a lock of her hair, saved trimmings from her fingernails, and tried to pull out one of her teeth.

Could YOU have been kidnapped by aliens without knowing it? Check the symptoms below. All have been reported by claimed victims of alien abduction:

- Nightmares about aliens

- Puzzling illnesses, such as headaches, feeling sick, or being unable to sleep

- Missing time, when you can't remember where you've been for whole periods at a stretch

- Unexplained scars or bruises

- Feeling of having flown through the air without knowing why or how

- Strange black marks that show up on an X-ray of your body

- Memories of flashing lights or being covered in liquid.

▲ Forced medical examinations are a common theme in abduction stories. In 1957, Brazilian farmer Antonio Villas Boas claimed he was snatched by aliens, stripped, and covered in a strange jelly before being forced to give blood.

UFO Down!

On July 4, 1947, Mac Brazel, a rancher living near Roswell, New Mexico, heard a loud explosion during a lightning storm. Checking his sheep the next day, he discovered a long rut and a trail of strange wreckage in the desert. It was "like nothing made on Earth"!

▼ The US Air Force wanted everyone to forget about the UFO crash. Why? One reason may have been to protect US national security. In 1947, the nearby Roswell air base was home to the world's only bomber planes armed with nuclear weapons.

When Brazel reported the trail of metal pieces to the local air base, he was arrested while the "flying disc" was retrieved. A few days later, another local man, Grady Barnett, claimed he had found a crashed UFO and the bodies of four aliens. These were also whisked away by the US Air Force. The official story was that the wreckage was nothing more than debris from a radar-tracking balloon. It was clearly a cover-up – but of what?

In 1996, a short film was released, showing what appeared to be the body of one of the aliens killed in the Roswell crash. In the film, supposedly made in 1947, two doctors carry out an autopsy on the alien, slicing open its chest and belly and removing its bizarre looking organs.

The doctors then cut the alien's skull in half to examine its brain. But medical experts who saw the film said the alien's injuries, including a deep cut in its right leg, could not have been from a plane crash. The film was later revealed to be a hoax.

▲ In 2006, the makers of the alien autopsy film revealed that they had created the alien body using body parts from chickens and pigs and a sheep's brain coated in raspberry jam!

Secrets of Area 51

At the time of the Roswell crash, many believed that the alien bodies had been taken to a top-security site known as Hangar 18 at Wright Patterson Air Force Base in Ohio. Some claim they are now stored in the mysterious Area 51, a top-secret air force base in Nevada, believed to be a center for US government research into UFOs and aliens.

Officially, Area 51 is a test base for new aircraft such as the U-2 and S-71 Blackbird spyplanes. If the US Air Force wanted to copy some of the technology from an alien spacecraft, this would be the perfect place to do it!

▼ Intense secrecy surrounds Area 51. This sign warns members of the public not to approach the site.

RESTRICTED AREA
NO TRESPASSING
BEYOND THIS POINT
WARNING
PHOTOGRAPHY IS PROHIBITED

Men in Black

Is there a government cover-up to keep us from finding out the truth about aliens? Yes, according to many UFO believers. How else to explain the sinister "Men in Black" who reportedly show up after UFO sightings and scare witnesses into silence?

The first story about men in black appeared in a book by author Gray Barker in 1956. In it, leading ufologist Albert Bender claimed that three men wearing dark suits had ordered him to stop publishing stories about UFOs. Scared to death, Bender agreed to give up his work. Later, Barker admitted that the story was made up, but strange tales about the "MIB" continued to circulate. In 1965, California accident investigator Rex Heflin took photos showing what he claimed was a hat-shaped UFO hovering over a road in Orange County. Shortly afterwards, Heflin was visited by men claiming to be from NORAD, the US government agency for aerospace defense, who demanded he hand over the photos. Who *were* these murky men?

In 1986, the pilot of a Japanese 747 airliner spotted a giant UFO over Alaska, which showed up on both air and ground radar. An investigation was carried out, and a report made to US President Reagan's Scientific Study Group. At the briefing, group members were told by a CIA agent they "were never there, and this never happened."

▼ *Many suspect that the US Defense Department, the Pentagon, knows a lot more about UFOs than it tells the public.*

MIB: The Theories

UFO Enforcers?

Many people believe that men in black are government agents tasked with keeping the rest of us in the dark about aliens. There's some evidence for this. In March 1967, a leaked memo from a senior US general revealed that unknown individuals really had been harrassing UFO witnesses, warning them not to talk and confiscating photos and film of UFO sightings.

Undercover Aliens?

If you believe the stories, the MIB often behave strangely, giggling out loud or creeping around furtively. One explanation is that they are really aliens or androids controlled by aliens, who have been sent to Earth to cover up alien activity. If that's the case, it still doesn't explain where they bought those suits!

Just a Hoax?

Many people say the whole idea of men in black is just a hoax dreamed up by authors like Gray Barker to sell more books.

But could the MIB be real? No one knows for certain. Another theory is that they may be US Air Force investigators tracking possible terrorists, or even spies who want to get their hands on the latest military hardware.

TOP SECRET
EYES ONLY

THE WHITE HOUSE
WASHINGTON

September 24, 1947

MEMORANDUM FOR THE SECRETARY OF DEFENSE

Dear Secretary Forrestal,

As per our recent conversation on this matter, you are hereby authorized to proceed with all due speed and caution on your undertaking. Hereafter this matter shall be referred to only as Operation Majestic Twelve.

It continues to be my feeling that any future considerations relative to the ultimate disposition of this matter should rest solely with the Office of the President following appropriate discussions with yourself, Dr. Bush and the Director of Central Intelligence.

Harry Truman

◄ In 1984, a secret document was discovered linking US President Harry Truman to the supposed crash of the alien spaceship near Roswell, New Mexico, in July 1947. In it, Truman sets up a committee of experts, the Majestic Twelve, to investigate the incident. But the fake letter was typed on a machine not invented until 1963!

War of the Worlds

They're coming – our planet is doomed! An alien invasion of Earth is every science fiction writer's favorite nightmare. What chance would we puny humans have against their superior technology and awesome firepower?

▲ *Many films have imagined a world where giant alien machines blast buildings and people to smithereens with powerful lasers. In John Wyndham's* The Day of the Triffids *(1951), man-eating plants take over the world!*

Strange explosions have been seen erupting on Mars. Then a blazing meteor thumps into the ground near your home.

You're one of the first on the scene. It's no meteor, but a long cylinder manned by a gruesome octopus-like creature. Suddenly, a powerful heat ray leaps out, burning everything in its path to a cinder. The army goes into action, but their primitive weapons are no match for the Martians' three-legged fighting machines, the Tripods.

More cylinders land. Within weeks the Tripods have conquered the world. While the Martians hunt down the survivors and feed on their blood, a red weed creeps across Earth, choking its plants.

All hope seems gone when you see a group of crows pecking at the body of a dead Martian. It's been poisoned by a tiny enemy – a type of bacteria to which the aliens have no resistance. By a miracle, Earth is saved!

◄ *This was how science fiction writer H.G. Wells (1866-1946) imagined an alien invasion in his famous book* The War of the Worlds.

Martian Attack!

In October 1938, actor Orson Welles presented a radio version of *The War of the Worlds*. His idea was to present events as if they were actually happening. The trouble was, he made it too realistic. When Welles warned that the Martians were heading for New York, people all over America believed him, jumped into their cars, and fled!

◄ *Orson Welles' version of* The War of the Worlds *was like a news broadcast, with reports of alien attacks coming in from all over the United States. No wonder listeners panicked!*

"Vast spider-like machines, nearly a hundred feet high, capable of the speed of an express train, and able to shoot out beams of intense heat..."
From The War of the Worlds *(1898) by H.G. Wells*

Riddles and Mysteries

Could aliens from outer space have left their mark on planet Earth? Many believe that extraterrestrials have been visiting Earth since the dawn of time. In fact, according to some, the signs of alien activity are all around – if you know where to look. Could there be a UFO hot spot near you?

Who Killed the Cows?

Among the freakiest events linked to aliens are the worldwide reports of cattle killed in bizarre ways. It's weird enough that the dead animals have had the blood drained from their bodies. But body parts such as eyes or lips have also been removed, while bits of flesh have been burnt at temperatures of up to 302°F (150°C).

Equally puzzling is the fact that there are no tracks of vehicles or footprints leading to or from the scene. Strange lights have often been sighted in the sky nearby. Ranchers have even reported seeing UFOs abducting their cattle. But can the reports really be believed? Could aliens have killed the cows? And if so, why?

▼ Most would say that natural predators are to blame for the cattle attacks. It's true that hunting birds like vultures go for soft body parts like lips and eyes first. But this doesn't explain the clean, precise cuts or the burns.

All sorts of weird occurrences have been blamed on UFOs. In 1981, French farmer Renato Nicolaï found "landing marks" in his garden made, he claimed, by the burning jets of a flying saucer.

For the last 30 years, strange lights have been seen over the valleys of Hessdalen in Norway. Scientists have tracked the lights with radar, infrared cameras and other instruments, but the source of the lights remains a mystery.

One of the most famous UFO hot spots is near Warminster in England. For over 20 years, strange patterns appeared overnight in fields of wheat and other crops. Some of these crop circles were almost 100 feet (30 m) wide. One expert blamed tornadoes – but others pointed the finger at flying saucers.

▼ *In 1991, hoaxers Doug Bower and Dave Chorley showed how they made the circles found at Warminster and elsewhere, using wooden planks, rope, and wire. But not all crop circles are so easy to explain…*

Have strange things being going on in YOUR area? Watch out for reports of lights in the sky, unexplained attacks on humans or animals, and mysterious disappearances – could they be the result of alien abductions? Keep a diary and collect cuttings from your local paper.

Ancient Astronauts

Have aliens been visiting us for thousands of years? Some people think so. They believe ETs shared their knowledge of science with early civilizations, forever changing the course of human history. But is there any proof?

Delve into ancient folklore and you'll find countless stories about "peoples from the skies." The Dogon people of Mali, Africa, claim they were taught about the stars by space beings called Nommo.

The UFO reports don't stop. In 590 BC, the prophet Ezekiel took seven days to recover after seeing a "great cloud with brightness around it and fire flashing forth." In 1566, a witness in Basel, Switzerland, described "black globes" moving across the sky at great speed and turning against each other "as if fighting."

▼ *Over 1,500 years ago, the ancient Peruvians drew lines and vast animal figures in the flat desert floor. But these figures can only been seen fully from the air. Could this be some giant UFO spaceport?*

▼ *Easter Island in the Pacific Ocean is one of the most remote islands on Earth. Yet it is covered with hundreds of giant Moai statues, each weighing several tons and some standing more than 30 feet (9 m) tall. Were they carved with a little alien help?*

Mysteries from the Dawn of Time

◄ Stonehenge is a remarkable Stone Age monument in Wiltshire, England, built around 2,500 BC. It's been suggested that the rings of giant standing stones, an aid to stargazing, were built to look like an alien flying saucer!

Some ancient paintings seem to show alien astronauts. In Australian Aboriginal folklore, the world was created by spirits called Wandjina who traveled to Earth from other worlds in flying "eggs" (spacecraft). Some Wandjina paintings show figures with halos around their head. Could these be alien space helmets?

In 1968, Swiss writer Erich von Däniken claimed that alien astronauts once visited Earth and helped to build great monuments such as the Egyptian pyramids and Stonehenge. Most of his ideas have since been proved wrong. Historians have shown that large gangs of skilled workers could have built the monuments using ropes, wooden rollers, and ramps.

▲ The Egyptian pyramids were built around the same time as Stonehenge from massive stones weighing many tons – and with great precision. They are also said to line up with the three stars in the constellation of Orion. Could their construction be another sign of alien meddling?

"[Ancient peoples] chisel in the rock pictures of what they had once seen: shapeless giants, with helmets and rods on their heads… rays are shot out as if from a sun; strange shapes, resembling giant insects, which were vehicles of some sort."

from Chariots of the Gods (1968), *by Erich von Däniken*

Alien Science

Not long ago, death rays, teletransporters, and invisibility cloaks were the stuff of science fiction. But with real-life scientists pushing back the boundaries all the time, some of the ideas dreamed up by sci-fi writers may not be quite so farfetched after all…

▶ To survive the long journeys across space, aliens might have to freeze their bodies. Some 150 or so human bodies have already been frozen in liquid nitrogen, in the hope that one day science will discover a way to bring them back to life.

What do YOU think aliens would look like?

- Weird-looking superhumans?
- Freaky animals with scaly skin, vicious fangs, and acid blood?
- Tiny creatures that worm into our bodies and take them over?
- Robot explorers or invaders?

Science Fact or Science Fiction?

Abductees are beamed on board an alien spacecraft in a ray of light...

Fact: In 2009, scientists discovered how to use light pressure from laser beams to move very small objects like cells. So a more advanced technology that allows aliens to "beam up" an unwilling victim may be a possibility.

A laser beam wipes out a whole city...

Fact: The US Air Force has already developed an airborne laser weapon system known as the Advanced Tactical Laser, which was fired for the first time in 2009. The High Frequency Active Auroral Research Program (HAARP) is a secret US project to build a superpowerful radio transmitter, which some people fear might have the power to fry the brains of a whole city!

UFOs disappear under a cloak of invisibility...

Fact: In 2010, a team of scientists produced a cloak made from tiny materials coated in silver that guided infrared light waves around an object, so that it almost entirely disappeared from view. If aliens have the technology to travel halfway across the galaxy, then an invisibility shield should be no problem!

Alien-human hybrid species are created by mingling human and alien DNA...

Fact: Genetic engineering is already with us – and it's here to stay. By mingling genes, scientists have been able to produce cats that glow in ultraviolet light and pigs whose organs can be transplanted into humans. So the idea of aliens changing their bodies to look like humans doesn't seem so fantastic.

Watching the Skies

Why not try some UFO hunting yourself? Make a regular skywatch from a hill or open space. Write down as many details as you can, and try to take a photo of any unusual objects flying overhead. Be warned, aliens aren't fussy about where they land!

UFOs aren't called "phantoms of the night" for nothing. It can be very hard to prove a genuine sighting. Often pictures of UFOs are fuzzy, or the saucer appears too far off to be identified with any certainty – so it helps to take friends along who can confirm what you've seen.

Do watch carefully – planes, meteors, and old satellites falling through the sky can easily be mistaken for flying saucers. So can the planets Venus or Jupiter shining brightly in the night sky.

If you do get lucky and a UFO appears nearby, remember to run away from it as fast as you can. You wouldn't want to be abducted by aliens...

▼ *Nighttime UFOs are called "nocturnal lights" while daytime UFOs are called "daylight discs." Whenever you head out, be sure to take the right gadgets with you. Here are some suggestions:*

UFO-WATCHING CHECKLIST
- Pen and paper for making notes
- Video camera
- Telescope
- Binoculars
- Star charts
- Maps
- Mobile phone
- Device for speedy Internet research
- Infrared thermal-imaging equipment for very dark nights
- Night-vision goggles

UFOs: Where to Look

Researchers have noticed that UFO sightings tend to come in waves that happen every few years. Often these occur in particular places, lasting anywhere from a few days to a couple of weeks.

- There have been more UFO sightings in Brazil than any other country in the world.

- The supposed alien crash landing near Roswell, New Mexico, is just one of many mysterious events reported in the notorious "Texas Triangle."

- The Nullarbor Plain, a vast treeless desert in southwestern Australia, is a focus of intense UFO activity.

- A remote area near the Ural mountains in Russia is known as the "M-triangle." Locals here have reported everything from strange lights and signs written in the sky to glowing aliens in the forest.

If you do see a UFO, you're in good company:

"It was big, it was very bright, it changed colors and it was about the size of the moon."

Jimmy Carter, US President, 1977–81

"I was in a plane last week when I looked out the window and saw this white light. It was zigzagging around… We followed it for several minutes."

Ronald Reagan, US President, 1981–89

"There was something out there that, uh, was close enough to be observed and what could it be… [it] had a series of ellipses, but when you made it real sharp, it was sort of L-shaped."

Buzz Aldrin, US astronaut

Don't just look at the sky! Strange metal objects have appeared in seas and lakes all over the world. These underwater craft are called Unidentified Submarine Objects (USOs). In 1980, over 70 people reported watching a 15-foot (4.5 m) metallic object rise from the Araguari River in Brazil, hover above their heads, then shoot off into the distance.

Twilight Quiz

Could YOU join the team at MIB as a special alien investigator? Try this easy-to-answer MIB recruitment quiz!

1. You spot strange flashing lights in the sky. Should you:

   a Blast those pesky flying saucers out of the sky with a surface-to-air missile?

   b Shoot as much video footage as you can, making detailed notes on what you see?

   c Put your hands over your eyes and count to ten? Hopefully the lights will be gone by then.

2. A local rancher reports that one of his cattle has been horribly mutilated. Do you:

   a Hide yourself inside the carcass and wait to ambush the aliens when they return for another juicy steak?

   b Take note of anything unusual, such as burn marks from landing spacecraft, unusually precise cuts, or strange footprints near the carcass?

   c Throw up over the crime scene?

3. You're asked to interview someone who believes they've been abducted by aliens. What do you say?

   a "Tell me every last gory detail. When we catch up with these guys, they're going to pay."

   b "Was anyone else there when this happened? Is there any physical evidence of what they did to you?"

   c "Just write it all down on this form. That weird stuff just freaks me out."

4. You're looking into the cold, glassy eyes of a real, live alien. What next?

   a Shoot first, ask questions later. ET and his friends need to realize that if they're looking for a new home, Earth is already taken.

   b Find a way to communicate with the alien visitor, using head and hand movements, lights, or sounds.

   c Run through the streets, screaming that an alien invasion is underway.

5. The MIB radio dish picks up a signal from deep space that might belong to an alien civilization. Do you:

   a Broadcast loud rock music back at them to scare them off?

   b Analyze the signal to look for patterns that might help you understand the alien code?

   c Go home and start packing. If the aliens are coming, it's time to take to the hills!

CHECK YOUR SCORE

Mostly 'a's Sorry, you're too trigger-happy for this job. But if the aliens invade, we'll give you a call.

Mostly 'b's You're brave but levelheaded – welcome to the team!

Mostly 'c's This job may not be for you. You'd be spooked by a flying Frisbee!

Glossary

abduction taking somebody away against their will

Aboriginal describing the earliest known inhabitants of Australia

aerobatic describing a skilled flying maneuver performed for an audience on the ground

aerospace industry dealing with space flight and aviation

androids robots that look like humans

autopsy a medical examination carried out on a dead body

bacterium a tiny organism that can carry disease

chisel to carve wood or stone using a special tool

cinder a piece of burnt coal or wood

colonize to take over and rule the population of a country

committee a group of people who meet for a special purpose

confiscate to take away or seize

constellation a group of stars

cosmos the planets and stars that make up the universe

extraterrestrial (ET) an alien; literally, something that comes from "outside the Earth"

firepower guns and other weapons

folklore traditional stories, beliefs, and customs

furtively in a secretive or suspicious way

galaxy a network of millions or billions of stars

goblin a dwarflike creature

gruesome horrible, revolting

harass to pester, threaten, or frighten somebody

hoax a deliberate plan to trick or fool people

Glossary (continued)

hybrid something made by combining two different elements

hypnosis putting somebody into a sleepy or dreamlike state

infrared invisible light given off by heated objects

jargon technical language that may not be understood by ordinary people

laser an intense, powerful beam of light

meteor a lump of rock or matter that flies through space

nocturnal occurring at night

nomads people who have no fixed home but travel from place to place

predator a creature that hunts others for food

puny weak or powerless

radar device for locating and tracking ships, planes, or other craft

rancher a person who runs a large cattle farm

satellite a spacecraft or object that orbits Earth

scholar a person who has made a special study of a field or subject

thermal imaging technique of photographing the heat given off by an object

tornado a type of whirlwind

ufologist a person who studies UFOs

ultraviolet a type of light found in sunlight but invisible to the human eye

undercover working in disguise or in secret

vulture a large hunting bird that feeds on dead animals

X-ray a special photograph that reveals organs inside the body

Further Reading and Websites

Further Reading

Aliens: An Owner's Guide, Jonathan Emmett (Macmillan Children's Books)

The Alien Hunter's Guide, Gomer Bolstrood (Edge series, Franklin Watts)

UFOs, David Orme (Trailblazers series, Ransom Publishing)

UFOs and Aliens, Anne Rooney (Amazing Mysteries series, Franklin Watts)

Aliens and UFOs, Christopher Evans (Carlton Books)

Unsolved! Mysteries of Alien Visitors and Abductions, Kathryn Walker (Crabtree Publishing Company)

The Unexplained: Encounters with Ghosts, Monsters and Aliens, Jim Pipe (Ticktock Media Ltd.)

Websites

www.nuforc.org
A site where you can register your own UFO sightings.

www.top10ufo.com
A good selection of pictures and videos of UFOs.

www.ufoevidence.org
Eyewitness accounts and photographs of UFOs.

http://ufostoday.com/
A website with news of aliens and UFO sightings.

http://www.seti.org/
The website of the Search for Extraterrestrial Intelligence Institute in Mountain View, California.

http://www.ufocasebook.com/Astronaut.html/
This website includes case studies of UFO sightings reported by astronauts.

http://sd4kids.skepdic.com/ufos.html/
An explanation of what scientists say about aliens and UFOs.

Index